This planner belongs to :

_____

Twenty-three

January

S	M	T	W	T	F	S
1	2	3	4	5	6	7
8	9	10	11	12	13	14
15	16	17	18	19	20	21
22	23	24	25	26	27	28
29	30	31				

February

S	M	T	W	T	F	S
			1	2	3	4
5	6	7	8	9	10	11
12	13	14	15	16	17	18
19	20	21	22	23	24	25
26	27	28				

March

S	M	T	W	T	F	S
			1	2	3	4
5	6	7	8	9	10	11
12	13	14	15	16	17	18
19	20	21	22	23	24	25
26	27	28	29	30	31	

April

S	M	T	W	T	F	S
						1
2	3	4	5	6	7	8
9	10	11	12	13	14	15
16	17	18	19	20	21	22
23	24	25	26	27	28	29
30						

May

S	M	T	W	T	F	S
	1	2	3	4	5	6
7	8	9	10	11	12	13
14	15	16	17	18	19	20
21	22	23	24	25	26	27
28	29	30	31			

June

S	M	T	W	T	F	S
				1	2	3
4	5	6	7	8	9	10
11	12	13	14	15	16	17
18	19	20	21	22	23	24
25	26	27	28	29	30	

July

S	M	T	W	T	F	S
						1
2	3	4	5	6	7	8
9	10	11	12	13	14	15
16	17	18	19	20	21	22
23	24	25	26	27	28	29
30	31					

August

S	M	T	W	T	F	S
		1	2	3	4	5
6	7	8	9	10	11	12
13	14	15	16	17	18	19
20	21	22	23	24	25	26
27	28	29	30	31		

September

S	M	T	W	T	F	S
					1	2
3	4	5	6	7	8	9
10	11	12	13	14	15	16
17	18	19	20	21	22	23
24	25	26	27	28	29	30

October

S	M	T	W	T	F	S
1	2	3	4	5	6	7
8	9	10	11	12	13	14
15	16	17	18	19	20	21
22	23	24	25	26	27	28
29	30	31				

November

S	M	T	W	T	F	S
			1	2	3	4
5	6	7	8	9	10	11
12	13	14	15	16	17	18
19	20	21	22	23	24	25
26	27	28	29	30		

December

S	M	T	W	T	F	S
					1	2
3	4	5	6	7	8	9
10	11	12	13	14	15	16
17	18	19	20	21	22	23
24	25	26	27	28	29	30
31						

Year in Pixels

	J	F	M	A	M	J	J	A	S	O	N	D
1.												
2.												
3.												
4.												
5.												
6.												
7.												
8.												
9.												
10.												
11.												
12.												
13.												
14.												
15.												
16.												
17.												
18.												
19.												
20.												
21.												
22.												
23.												
24.												
25.												
26.												
27.												
28.												
29.												
30.												
31.												

Color Codes

Notes

January

2023

MONDAY	TUESDAY	WEDNESDAY	THURSDAY
2	3	4	5
9	10	11	12
16	17	18	19
23	24	25	26

January

2023

FRIDAY	SATURDAY	SUNDAY	NOTES
		1	○
			○
			○
			○
			○
6	7	8	○
			○
			○
			○
13	14	15	○
			○
			○
			○
			○
20	21	22	○
			○
			○
			○
			○
27	28	29	30 / 31

February \ 2023

MONDAY	TUESDAY	WEDNESDAY	THURSDAY
		1	2
6	7	8	9
13	14	15	16
20	21	22	23
27	28		

February

FRIDAY	SATURDAY	SUNDAY	NOTES
3	4	5	○
			○
			○
			○
			○
10	11	12	○
			○
			○
			○
17	18	19	○
			○
			○
			○
			○
24	25	26	○
			○
			○
			○
			○
			NOTES

March

2023

MONDAY	TUESDAY	WEDNESDAY	THURSDAY
		1	2
6	7	8	9
13	14	15	16
20	21	22	23
27	28	29	30

March

FRIDAY	SATURDAY	SUNDAY	NOTES
3	4	5	○
			○
			○
			○
			○
10	11	12	○
			○
			○
			○
17	18	19	○
			○
			○
			○
			○
24	25	26	○
			○
			○
			○
			○
31			NOTES

April

MONDAY	TUESDAY	WEDNESDAY	THURSDAY
3	4	5	6
10	11	12	13
17	18	19	20
24	25	26	27

April

FRIDAY	SATURDAY	SUNDAY	NOTES
	1	2	○
			○
			○
			○
			○
7	8	9	○
			○
			○
			○
14	15	16	○
			○
			○
			○
			○
21	22	23	○
			○
			○
			○
			○
28	29	30	NOTES

May

2023

MONDAY	TUESDAY	WEDNESDAY	THURSDAY
1	2	3	4
8	9	10	11
15	16	17	18
22	23	24	25
29	30	31	

May

2023

FRIDAY	SATURDAY	SUNDAY	NOTES
5	6	7	○
			○
			○
			○
			○
12	13	14	○
			○
			○
			○
19	20	21	○
			○
			○
			○
			○
26	27	28	○
			○
			○
			○
			○
			NOTES

June
2023

MONDAY	TUESDAY	WEDNESDAY	THURSDAY
			1
5	6	7	8
12	13	14	15
19	20	21	22
26	27	28	29

June

FRIDAY	SATURDAY	SUNDAY	NOTES
2	3	4	○
			○
			○
			○
			○
9	10	11	○
			○
			○
			○
16	17	18	○
			○
			○
			○
			○
23	24	25	○
			○
			○
			○
			○
30			NOTES

July

MONDAY	TUESDAY	WEDNESDAY	THURSDAY
3	4	5	6
10	11	12	13
17	18	19	20
24	25	26	27

July

2023

FRIDAY	SATURDAY	SUNDAY	NOTES
	1	2	○
			○
			○
			○
			○
7	8	9	○
			○
			○
			○
14	15	16	○
			○
			○
			○
			○
21	22	23	○
			○
			○
			○
			○
28	29	30	31

August 2023

MONDAY	TUESDAY	WEDNESDAY	THURSDAY
	1	2	3
7	8	9	10
14	15	16	17
21	22	23	24
28	29	30	31

August

2023

FRIDAY	SATURDAY	SUNDAY	NOTES
4	5	6	○
			○
			○
			○
			○
11	12	13	○
			○
			○
			○
18	19	20	○
			○
			○
			○
			○
25	26	27	NOTES

September 2023

MONDAY	TUESDAY	WEDNESDAY	THURSDAY
4	5	6	7
11	12	13	14
18	19	20	21
25	26	27	28

September

FRIDAY	SATURDAY	SUNDAY	NOTES
1	2	3	○
			○
			○
			○
			○
8	9	10	○
			○
			○
			○
15	16	17	○
			○
			○
			○
			○
22	23	24	○
			○
			○
			○
			○
29	30		NOTES

October

MONDAY	TUESDAY	WEDNESDAY	THURSDAY
2	3	4	5
9	10	11	12
16	17	18	19
23	24	25	26

October

FRIDAY	SATURDAY	SUNDAY	NOTES
		1	○
			○
			○
			○
			○
6	7	8	○
			○
			○
			○
13	14	15	○
			○
			○
			○
			○
20	21	22	○
			○
			○
			○
			○
27	28	29	30 / 31

November 2023

MONDAY	TUESDAY	WEDNESDAY	THURSDAY
		1	2
6	7	8	9
13	14	15	16
20	21	22	23
27	28	29	30

November

FRIDAY	SATURDAY	SUNDAY	NOTES
3	4	5	○
			○
			○
			○
			○
10	11	12	○
			○
			○
			○
17	18	19	○
			○
			○
			○
			○
24	25	26	○
			○
			○
			○
			○
			NOTES

December 2023

MONDAY	TUESDAY	WEDNESDAY	THURSDAY
4	5	6	7
11	12	13	14
18	19	20	21
25	26	27	28

December

FRIDAY	SATURDAY	SUNDAY	NOTES
1	2	3	○
			○
			○
			○
			○
8	9	10	○
			○
			○
			○
15	16	17	○
			○
			○
			○
			○
22	23	24	○
			○
			○
			○
			○
29	30	31	NOTES

December
2022

01 THURSDAY

○ _____
○ _____
○ _____
○ _____
○ _____
○ _____
○ _____
○ _____

02 FRIDAY

○ _____
○ _____
○ _____
○ _____
○ _____
○ _____
○ _____
○ _____

03 SATURDAY

○ _____
○ _____
○ _____
○ _____
○ _____
○ _____
○ _____
○ _____

04 SUNDAY

○ _____
○ _____
○ _____
○ _____
○ _____

05 MONDAY

-
-
-
-
-
-
-
-

06 TUESDAY

-
-
-
-
-
-
-
-

07 WEDNESDAY

-
-
-
-
-
-
-
-

08 THURSDAY

-
-
-
-
-

09 FRIDAY

○ _____
○ _____
○ _____
○ _____
○ _____
○ _____
○ _____
○ _____

10 SATURDAY

○ _____
○ _____
○ _____
○ _____
○ _____
○ _____
○ _____
○ _____

11 SUNDAY

○ _____
○ _____
○ _____
○ _____
○ _____
○ _____
○ _____
○ _____

12 MONDAY

○ _____
○ _____
○ _____
○ _____
○ _____

13 TUESDAY

○ _____
○ _____
○ _____
○ _____
○ _____
○ _____
○ _____
○ _____

14 WEDNESDAY

○ _____
○ _____
○ _____
○ _____
○ _____
○ _____
○ _____
○ _____

15 THURSDAY

○ _____
○ _____
○ _____
○ _____
○ _____
○ _____
○ _____
○ _____

16 FRIDAY

○ _____
○ _____
○ _____
○ _____
○ _____

17 SATURDAY

○
○
○
○
○
○
○
○

18 SUNDAY

○
○
○
○
○
○
○
○

19 MONDAY

○
○
○
○
○
○
○
○

20 TUESDAY

○
○
○
○
○

21 WEDNESDAY

○
○
○
○
○
○
○
○

22 THURSDAY

○
○
○
○
○
○
○
○

23 FRIDAY

○
○
○
○
○
○
○
○

24 SATURDAY

○
○
○
○
○

25 SUNDAY

○
○
○
○
○
○
○
○

26 MONDAY

○
○
○
○
○
○
○
○

27 TUESDAY

○
○
○
○
○
○
○
○

28 WEDNESDAY

○
○
○
○
○

December
2022

29 THURSDAY
○
○
○
○
○
○
○
○

30 FRIDAY
○
○
○
○
○
○
○
○

31 SATURDAY
○
○
○
○
○
○
○
○

NOTES

January
2023

01 SUNDAY

○ _____
○ _____
○ _____
○ _____
○ _____
○ _____
○ _____
○ _____

02 MONDAY

○ _____
○ _____
○ _____
○ _____
○ _____
○ _____
○ _____
○ _____

03 TUESDAY

○ _____
○ _____
○ _____
○ _____
○ _____
○ _____
○ _____
○ _____

04 WEDNESDAY

○ _____
○ _____
○ _____
○ _____
○ _____

January
2023

05 THURSDAY

- ○
- ○
- ○
- ○
- ○
- ○
- ○
- ○

06 FRIDAY

- ○
- ○
- ○
- ○
- ○
- ○
- ○
- ○

07 SATURDAY

- ○
- ○
- ○
- ○
- ○
- ○
- ○
- ○

08 SUNDAY

- ○
- ○
- ○
- ○
- ○

January
2023

09 MONDAY

○ _____
○ _____
○ _____
○ _____
○ _____
○ _____
○ _____
○ _____

10 TUESDAY

○ _____
○ _____
○ _____
○ _____
○ _____
○ _____
○ _____
○ _____

11 WEDNESDAY

○ _____
○ _____
○ _____
○ _____
○ _____
○ _____
○ _____
○ _____

12 THURSDAY

○ _____
○ _____
○ _____
○ _____
○ _____

13 FRIDAY

○
○
○
○
○
○
○
○

14 SATURDAY

○
○
○
○
○
○
○
○

15 SUNDAY

○
○
○
○
○
○
○
○

16 MONDAY

○
○
○
○
○

January 2023

17 TUESDAY

○ _____
○ _____
○ _____
○ _____
○ _____
○ _____
○ _____
○ _____

18 WEDNESDAY

○ _____
○ _____
○ _____
○ _____
○ _____
○ _____
○ _____
○ _____

19 THURSDAY

○ _____
○ _____
○ _____
○ _____
○ _____
○ _____
○ _____
○ _____

20 FRIDAY

○ _____
○ _____
○ _____
○ _____
○ _____

21 SATURDAY

○ _____
○ _____
○ _____
○ _____
○ _____
○ _____
○ _____
○ _____

22 SUNDAY

○ _____
○ _____
○ _____
○ _____
○ _____
○ _____
○ _____
○ _____

23 MONDAY

○ _____
○ _____
○ _____
○ _____
○ _____
○ _____
○ _____
○ _____

24 TUESDAY

○ _____
○ _____
○ _____
○ _____
○ _____

January

2023

25 WEDNESDAY

○
○
○
○
○
○
○
○

26 THURSDAY

○
○
○
○
○
○
○
○

27 FRIDAY

○
○
○
○
○
○
○
○

28 SATURDAY

○
○
○
○
○

January
2023

29 SUNDAY

- ○ _____
- ○ _____
- ○ _____
- ○ _____
- ○ _____
- ○ _____
- ○ _____
- ○ _____

30 MONDAY

- ○ _____
- ○ _____
- ○ _____
- ○ _____
- ○ _____
- ○ _____
- ○ _____
- ○ _____
- ○ _____

31 TUESDAY

- ○ _____
- ○ _____
- ○ _____
- ○ _____
- ○ _____
- ○ _____
- ○ _____
- ○ _____

NOTES

_____
_____
_____
_____

February
2023

01 WEDNESDAY

- ○
- ○
- ○
- ○
- ○
- ○
- ○
- ○

02 THURSDAY

- ○
- ○
- ○
- ○
- ○
- ○
- ○
- ○

03 FRIDAY

- ○
- ○
- ○
- ○
- ○
- ○
- ○
- ○

04 SATURDAY

- ○
- ○
- ○
- ○
- ○

February
2023

05 SUNDAY

○
○
○
○
○
○
○
○

06 MONDAY

○
○
○
○
○
○
○
○

07 TUESDAY

○
○
○
○
○
○
○
○

08 WEDNESDAY

○
○
○
○
○

February
2023

09 THURSDAY

○
○
○
○
○
○
○
○

10 FRIDAY

○
○
○
○
○
○
○
○

11 SATURDAY

○
○
○
○
○
○
○
○

12 SUNDAY

○
○
○
○
○

February
2023

13 MONDAY
○
○
○
○
○
○
○
○

14 TUESDAY
○
○
○
○
○
○
○
○

15 WEDNESDAY
○
○
○
○
○
○
○
○

16 THURSDAY
○
○
○
○
○

17 FRIDAY

○ _____
○ _____
○ _____
○ _____
○ _____
○ _____
○ _____
○ _____

18 SATURDAY

○ _____
○ _____
○ _____
○ _____
○ _____
○ _____
○ _____
○ _____

19 SUNDAY

○ _____
○ _____
○ _____
○ _____
○ _____
○ _____
○ _____
○ _____

20 MONDAY

○ _____
○ _____
○ _____
○ _____
○ _____

21 TUESDAY

○ _____
○ _____
○ _____
○ _____
○ _____
○ _____
○ _____
○ _____
○ _____

22 WEDNESDAY

○ _____
○ _____
○ _____
○ _____
○ _____
○ _____
○ _____
○ _____

23 THURSDAY

○ _____
○ _____
○ _____
○ _____
○ _____
○ _____
○ _____
○ _____

24 FRIDAY

○ _____
○ _____
○ _____
○ _____
○ _____

February
2023

25 SATURDAY

○
○
○
○
○
○
○
○

26 SUNDAY

○
○
○
○
○
○
○
○

27 MONDAY

○
○
○
○
○
○
○
○

28 TUESDAY

○
○
○
○
○

March 2023

01 WEDNESDAY

○ _____
○ _____
○ _____
○ _____
○ _____
○ _____
○ _____
○ _____

02 THURSDAY

○ _____
○ _____
○ _____
○ _____
○ _____
○ _____
○ _____
○ _____

03 FRIDAY

○ _____
○ _____
○ _____
○ _____
○ _____
○ _____
○ _____
○ _____

04 SATURDAY

○ _____
○ _____
○ _____
○ _____
○ _____

March
2023

05 SUNDAY

○
○
○
○
○
○
○
○

06 MONDAY

○
○
○
○
○
○
○
○

07 TUESDAY

○
○
○
○
○
○
○
○

08 WEDNESDAY

○
○
○
○
○

09 THURSDAY

○ _____
○ _____
○ _____
○ _____
○ _____
○ _____
○ _____
○ _____

10 FRIDAY

○ _____
○ _____
○ _____
○ _____
○ _____
○ _____
○ _____
○ _____

11 SATURDAY

○ _____
○ _____
○ _____
○ _____
○ _____
○ _____
○ _____
○ _____

12 SUNDAY

○ _____
○ _____
○ _____
○ _____
○ _____

13 MONDAY

○
○
○
○
○
○
○
○

14 TUESDAY

○
○
○
○
○
○
○
○

15 WEDNESDAY

○
○
○
○
○
○
○
○

16 THURSDAY

○
○
○
○
○

17 FRIDAY

○
○
○
○
○
○
○
○

18 SATURDAY

○
○
○
○
○
○
○
○

19 SUNDAY

○
○
○
○
○
○
○
○

20 MONDAY

○
○
○
○
○

21 TUESDAY

○
○
○
○
○
○
○
○

22 WEDNESDAY

○
○
○
○
○
○
○
○

23 THURSDAY

○
○
○
○
○
○
○
○

24 FRIDAY

○
○
○
○
○

25 SATURDAY

○
○
○
○
○
○
○
○

26 SUNDAY

○
○
○
○
○
○
○
○

27 MONDAY

○
○
○
○
○
○
○
○

28 TUESDAY

○
○
○
○
○

29 WEDNESDAY

○ _____
○ _____
○ _____
○ _____
○ _____
○ _____
○ _____
○ _____

30 THURSDAY

○ _____
○ _____
○ _____
○ _____
○ _____
○ _____
○ _____
○ _____

31 FRIDAY

○ _____
○ _____
○ _____
○ _____
○ _____
○ _____
○ _____
○ _____

NOTES

_____
_____
_____
_____

April 2023

01 SATURDAY

02 SUNDAY

03 MONDAY

04 TUESDAY

April
2023

05 WEDNESDAY

06 THURSDAY

07 FRIDAY

08 SATURDAY

09 SUNDAY

○ _____
○ _____
○ _____
○ _____
○ _____
○ _____
○ _____
○ _____

10 MONDAY

○ _____
○ _____
○ _____
○ _____
○ _____
○ _____
○ _____
○ _____

11 TUESDAY

○ _____
○ _____
○ _____
○ _____
○ _____
○ _____
○ _____
○ _____

12 WEDNESDAY

○ _____
○ _____
○ _____
○ _____
○ _____

13 THURSDAY

○
○
○
○
○
○
○
○

14 FRIDAY

○
○
○
○
○
○
○
○

15 SATURDAY

○
○
○
○
○
○
○
○

16 SUNDAY

○
○
○
○
○

17 MONDAY

○
○
○
○
○
○
○
○

18 TUESDAY

○
○
○
○
○
○
○
○

19 WEDNESDAY

○
○
○
○
○
○
○
○

20 THURSDAY

○
○
○
○
○

21 FRIDAY

○
○
○
○
○
○
○
○

22 SATURDAY

○
○
○
○
○
○
○
○

23 SUNDAY

○
○
○
○
○
○
○
○

24 MONDAY

○
○
○
○
○

25 TUESDAY

○
○
○
○
○
○
○
○

26 WEDNESDAY

○
○
○
○
○
○
○
○

27 THURSDAY

○
○
○
○
○
○
○
○

28 FRIDAY

○
○
○
○
○

29 SATURDAY

○ _____
○ _____
○ _____
○ _____
○ _____
○ _____
○ _____
○ _____

30 SUNDAY

○ _____
○ _____
○ _____
○ _____
○ _____
○ _____
○ _____
○ _____

NOTES

_____
_____
_____
_____
_____
_____
_____
_____
_____
_____
_____

01 MONDAY

○
○
○
○
○
○
○
○

02 TUESDAY

○
○
○
○
○
○
○
○

03 WEDNESDAY

○
○
○
○
○
○
○
○

04 THURSDAY

○
○
○
○
○

May
2023

05 FRIDAY
- ○
- ○
- ○
- ○
- ○
- ○
- ○
- ○

06 SATURDAY
- ○
- ○
- ○
- ○
- ○
- ○
- ○
- ○

07 SUNDAY
- ○
- ○
- ○
- ○
- ○
- ○
- ○
- ○

08 MONDAY
- ○
- ○
- ○
- ○
- ○

09 TUESDAY

○
○
○
○
○
○
○
○

10 WEDNESDAY

○
○
○
○
○
○
○
○

11 THURSDAY

○
○
○
○
○
○
○
○

12 FRIDAY

○
○
○
○
○

13 SATURDAY

○
○
○
○
○
○
○
○

14 SUNDAY

○
○
○
○
○
○
○
○

15 MONDAY

○
○
○
○
○
○
○
○

16 TUESDAY

○
○
○
○
○

17 WEDNESDAY

○
○
○
○
○
○
○
○

18 THURSDAY

○
○
○
○
○
○
○
○

19 FRIDAY

○
○
○
○
○
○
○
○

20 SATURDAY

○
○
○
○
○

21 SUNDAY

○
○
○
○
○
○
○
○

22 MONDAY

○
○
○
○
○
○
○
○

23 TUESDAY

○
○
○
○
○
○
○
○

24 WEDNESDAY

○
○
○
○
○

May
2023

25 THURSDAY

○
○
○
○
○
○
○
○

26 FRIDAY

○
○
○
○
○
○
○
○

27 SATURDAY

○
○
○
○
○
○
○
○

28 SUNDAY

○
○
○
○
○

May 2023

29 MONDAY
○
○
○
○
○
○
○
○

30 TUESDAY
○
○
○
○
○
○
○
○

31 WEDNESDAY
○
○
○
○
○
○
○
○

NOTES

June 2023

01 THURSDAY

- ○
- ○
- ○
- ○
- ○
- ○
- ○
- ○

02 FRIDAY

- ○
- ○
- ○
- ○
- ○
- ○
- ○
- ○

03 SATURDAY

- ○
- ○
- ○
- ○
- ○
- ○
- ○
- ○

04 SUNDAY

- ○
- ○
- ○
- ○
- ○

June
2023

05 MONDAY

○ _____
○ _____
○ _____
○ _____
○ _____
○ _____
○ _____
○ _____

06 TUESDAY

○ _____
○ _____
○ _____
○ _____
○ _____
○ _____
○ _____
○ _____

07 WEDNESDAY

○ _____
○ _____
○ _____
○ _____
○ _____
○ _____
○ _____
○ _____

08 THURSDAY

○ _____
○ _____
○ _____
○ _____
○ _____

09 FRIDAY

- ○
- ○
- ○
- ○
- ○
- ○
- ○
- ○

10 SATURDAY

- ○
- ○
- ○
- ○
- ○
- ○
- ○
- ○

11 SUNDAY

- ○
- ○
- ○
- ○
- ○
- ○
- ○
- ○

12 MONDAY

- ○
- ○
- ○
- ○
- ○

13 TUESDAY

○ _____
○ _____
○ _____
○ _____
○ _____
○ _____
○ _____
○ _____

14 WEDNESDAY

○ _____
○ _____
○ _____
○ _____
○ _____
○ _____
○ _____
○ _____

15 THURSDAY

○ _____
○ _____
○ _____
○ _____
○ _____
○ _____
○ _____
○ _____

16 FRIDAY

○ _____
○ _____
○ _____
○ _____
○ _____

17 SATURDAY

-
-
-
-
-
-
-
-

18 SUNDAY

-
-
-
-
-
-
-
-

19 MONDAY

-
-
-
-
-
-
-
-

20 TUESDAY

-
-
-
-
-

June
2023

21 WEDNESDAY

○
○
○
○
○
○
○
○

22 THURSDAY

○
○
○
○
○
○
○
○

23 FRIDAY

○
○
○
○
○
○
○
○

24 SATURDAY

○
○
○
○
○

June 2023

25 SUNDAY
- ○
- ○
- ○
- ○
- ○
- ○
- ○
- ○

26 MONDAY
- ○
- ○
- ○
- ○
- ○
- ○
- ○
- ○

27 TUESDAY
- ○
- ○
- ○
- ○
- ○
- ○
- ○
- ○

28 WEDNESDAY
- ○
- ○
- ○
- ○
- ○

29 THURSDAY

- ○
- ○
- ○
- ○
- ○
- ○
- ○
- ○

30 FRIDAY

- ○
- ○
- ○
- ○
- ○
- ○
- ○
- ○

NOTES

July 2023

01 SATURDAY
- ○
- ○
- ○
- ○
- ○
- ○
- ○
- ○

02 SUNDAY
- ○
- ○
- ○
- ○
- ○
- ○
- ○
- ○

03 MONDAY
- ○
- ○
- ○
- ○
- ○
- ○
- ○
- ○

04 TUESDAY
- ○
- ○
- ○
- ○
- ○

05 WEDNESDAY
○
○
○
○
○
○
○
○

06 THURSDAY
○
○
○
○
○
○
○
○

07 FRIDAY
○
○
○
○
○
○
○
○

08 SATURDAY
○
○
○
○
○

09 SUNDAY

○
○
○
○
○
○
○
○

10 MONDAY

○
○
○
○
○
○
○
○

11 TUESDAY

○
○
○
○
○
○
○
○

12 WEDNESDAY

○
○
○
○
○

13 THURSDAY

○
○
○
○
○
○
○
○

14 FRIDAY

○
○
○
○
○
○
○
○

15 SATURDAY

○
○
○
○
○
○
○
○

16 SUNDAY

○
○
○
○
○

17 MONDAY

○
○
○
○
○
○
○
○

18 TUESDAY

○
○
○
○
○
○
○
○

19 WEDNESDAY

○
○
○
○
○
○
○
○

20 THURSDAY

○
○
○
○
○

July
2023

21 FRIDAY

○ _____
○ _____
○ _____
○ _____
○ _____
○ _____
○ _____
○ _____

22 SATURDAY

○ _____
○ _____
○ _____
○ _____
○ _____
○ _____
○ _____
○ _____

23 SUNDAY

○ _____
○ _____
○ _____
○ _____
○ _____
○ _____
○ _____
○ _____

24 MONDAY

○ _____
○ _____
○ _____
○ _____
○ _____

25 TUESDAY

○
○
○
○
○
○
○
○

26 WEDNESDAY

○
○
○
○
○
○
○
○

27 THURSDAY

○
○
○
○
○
○
○
○

28 FRIDAY

○
○
○
○
○

July
2023

29 SATURDAY
- ○ _____
- ○ _____
- ○ _____
- ○ _____
- ○ _____
- ○ _____
- ○ _____
- ○ _____

30 SUNDAY
- ○ _____
- ○ _____
- ○ _____
- ○ _____
- ○ _____
- ○ _____
- ○ _____
- ○ _____

31 MONDAY
- ○ _____
- ○ _____
- ○ _____
- ○ _____
- ○ _____
- ○ _____
- ○ _____
- ○ _____

NOTES
_____
_____
_____
_____

01 TUESDAY
- ○
- ○
- ○
- ○
- ○
- ○
- ○
- ○

02 WEDNESDAY
- ○
- ○
- ○
- ○
- ○
- ○
- ○
- ○

03 THURSDAY
- ○
- ○
- ○
- ○
- ○
- ○
- ○
- ○

04 FRIDAY
- ○
- ○
- ○
- ○
- ○

August
2023

05 SATURDAY
- ○
- ○
- ○
- ○
- ○
- ○
- ○
- ○

06 SUNDAY
- ○
- ○
- ○
- ○
- ○
- ○
- ○
- ○

07 MONDAY
- ○
- ○
- ○
- ○
- ○
- ○
- ○
- ○

08 TUESDAY
- ○
- ○
- ○
- ○
- ○

09 WEDNESDAY

○
○
○
○
○
○
○
○

10 THURSDAY

○
○
○
○
○
○
○
○

11 FRIDAY

○
○
○
○
○
○
○
○

12 SATURDAY

○
○
○
○
○

August
2023

13 SUNDAY

14 MONDAY

15 TUESDAY

16 WEDNESDAY

17 THURSDAY

○
○
○
○
○
○
○
○

18 FRIDAY

○
○
○
○
○
○
○
○
○

19 SATURDAY

○
○
○
○
○
○
○
○

20 SUNDAY

○
○
○
○
○

21 MONDAY
- ○
- ○
- ○
- ○
- ○
- ○
- ○
- ○

22 TUESDAY
- ○
- ○
- ○
- ○
- ○
- ○
- ○
- ○

23 WEDNESDAY
- ○
- ○
- ○
- ○
- ○
- ○
- ○
- ○

24 THURSDAY
- ○
- ○
- ○
- ○
- ○

August 2023

25 FRIDAY

- ○
- ○
- ○
- ○
- ○
- ○
- ○
- ○

26 SATURDAY

- ○
- ○
- ○
- ○
- ○
- ○
- ○
- ○

27 SUNDAY

- ○
- ○
- ○
- ○
- ○
- ○
- ○
- ○

28 MONDAY

- ○
- ○
- ○
- ○
- ○

August
2023

29 TUESDAY

- ○
- ○
- ○
- ○
- ○
- ○
- ○
- ○

30 WEDNESDAY

- ○
- ○
- ○
- ○
- ○
- ○
- ○
- ○

31 THURSDAY

- ○
- ○
- ○
- ○
- ○
- ○
- ○
- ○

NOTES

01 FRIDAY

- ○
- ○
- ○
- ○
- ○
- ○
- ○
- ○

02 SATURDAY

- ○
- ○
- ○
- ○
- ○
- ○
- ○
- ○

03 SUNDAY

- ○
- ○
- ○
- ○
- ○
- ○
- ○
- ○

04 MONDAY

- ○
- ○
- ○
- ○
- ○

05 TUESDAY

○
○ _____
○ _____
○ _____
○ _____
○ _____
○ _____
○ _____

06 WEDNESDAY

○
○ _____
○ _____
○ _____
○ _____
○ _____
○ _____
○ _____

07 THURSDAY

○
○ _____
○ _____
○ _____
○ _____
○ _____
○ _____
○ _____

08 FRIDAY

○
○ _____
○ _____
○ _____
○ _____

09 SATURDAY

○ _____
○ _____
○ _____
○ _____
○ _____
○ _____
○ _____
○ _____

10 SUNDAY

○ _____
○ _____
○ _____
○ _____
○ _____
○ _____
○ _____
○ _____

11 MONDAY

○ _____
○ _____
○ _____
○ _____
○ _____
○ _____
○ _____
○ _____

12 TUESDAY

○ _____
○ _____
○ _____
○ _____
○ _____

September
2023

13 WEDNESDAY

○
○
○
○
○
○
○
○

14 THURSDAY

○
○
○
○
○
○
○
○

15 FRIDAY

○
○
○
○
○
○
○
○

16 SATURDAY

○
○
○
○
○

17 SUNDAY

18 MONDAY

19 TUESDAY

20 WEDNESDAY

21 THURSDAY

○ _____
○ _____
○ _____
○ _____
○ _____
○ _____
○ _____
○ _____

22 FRIDAY

○ _____
○ _____
○ _____
○ _____
○ _____
○ _____
○ _____
○ _____

23 SATURDAY

○ _____
○ _____
○ _____
○ _____
○ _____
○ _____
○ _____
○ _____

24 SUNDAY

○ _____
○ _____
○ _____
○ _____
○ _____

25 MONDAY

○
○
○
○
○
○
○
○

26 TUESDAY

○
○
○
○
○
○
○
○

27 WEDNESDAY

○
○
○
○
○
○
○
○

28 THURSDAY

○
○
○
○
○

September
2023

29 FRIDAY

○ _____
○ _____
○ _____
○ _____
○ _____
○ _____
○ _____
○ _____

30 SATURDAY

○ _____
○ _____
○ _____
○ _____
○ _____
○ _____
○ _____
○ _____

NOTES

_____
_____
_____
_____
_____
_____
_____
_____
_____
_____
_____
_____
_____

October
2023

01 SUNDAY

○
○
○
○
○
○
○
○

02 MONDAY

○
○
○
○
○
○
○
○

03 TUESDAY

○
○
○
○
○
○
○
○

04 WEDNESDAY

○
○
○
○
○

05 THURSDAY

○
○
○
○
○
○
○
○

06 FRIDAY

○
○
○
○
○
○
○
○

07 SATURDAY

○
○
○
○
○
○
○
○

08 SUNDAY

○
○
○
○
○

October
2023

09 MONDAY
- ○
- ○
- ○
- ○
- ○
- ○
- ○
- ○

10 TUESDAY
- ○
- ○
- ○
- ○
- ○
- ○
- ○
- ○

11 WEDNESDAY
- ○
- ○
- ○
- ○
- ○
- ○
- ○
- ○

12 THURSDAY
- ○
- ○
- ○
- ○
- ○

October

2023

13 FRIDAY

14 SATURDAY

15 SUNDAY

16 MONDAY

17 TUESDAY
- ○
- ○
- ○
- ○
- ○
- ○
- ○
- ○

18 WEDNESDAY
- ○
- ○
- ○
- ○
- ○
- ○
- ○
- ○

19 THURSDAY
- ○
- ○
- ○
- ○
- ○
- ○
- ○
- ○

20 FRIDAY
- ○
- ○
- ○
- ○
- ○

October
2023

21 SATURDAY
- ○
- ○
- ○
- ○
- ○
- ○
- ○
- ○

22 SUNDAY
- ○
- ○
- ○
- ○
- ○
- ○
- ○
- ○

23 MONDAY
- ○
- ○
- ○
- ○
- ○
- ○
- ○
- ○

24 TUESDAY
- ○
- ○
- ○
- ○
- ○

25 WEDNESDAY

○
○
○
○
○
○
○
○

26 THURSDAY

○
○
○
○
○
○
○
○

27 FRIDAY

○
○
○
○
○
○
○
○

28 SATURDAY

○
○
○
○
○

October
2023

29 SUNDAY
- ○
- ○
- ○
- ○
- ○
- ○
- ○
- ○

30 MONDAY
- ○
- ○
- ○
- ○
- ○
- ○
- ○
- ○

31 TUESDAY
- ○
- ○
- ○
- ○
- ○
- ○
- ○
- ○

NOTES

November
2023

01 WEDNESDAY

○
○
○
○
○
○
○
○

02 THURSDAY

○
○
○
○
○
○
○
○

03 FRIDAY

○
○
○
○
○
○
○
○

04 SATURDAY

○
○
○
○
○

November
2023

05 SUNDAY

○ _____
○ _____
○ _____
○ _____
○ _____
○ _____
○ _____
○ _____

06 MONDAY

○ _____
○ _____
○ _____
○ _____
○ _____
○ _____
○ _____
○ _____

07 TUESDAY

○ _____
○ _____
○ _____
○ _____
○ _____
○ _____
○ _____
○ _____

08 WEDNESDAY

○ _____
○ _____
○ _____
○ _____
○ _____

November
2023

09 THURSDAY

○
○
○
○
○
○
○
○

10 FRIDAY

○
○
○
○
○
○
○
○

11 SATURDAY

○
○
○
○
○
○
○
○

12 SUNDAY

○
○
○
○
○

13 MONDAY

○
_____
○
_____
○
_____
○
_____
○
_____
○
_____
○
_____
○
_____

14 TUESDAY

○
_____
○
_____
○
_____
○
_____
○
_____
○
_____
○
_____
○
_____

15 WEDNESDAY

○
_____
○
_____
○
_____
○
_____
○
_____
○
_____
○
_____
○
_____

16 THURSDAY

○
_____
○
_____
○
_____
○
_____
○
_____

17 FRIDAY

○
○
○
○
○
○
○
○

18 SATURDAY

○
○
○
○
○
○
○
○
○

19 SUNDAY

○
○
○
○
○
○
○
○

20 MONDAY

○
○
○
○
○

November
2023

21 TUESDAY
- ○
- ○
- ○
- ○
- ○
- ○
- ○
- ○

22 WEDNESDAY
- ○
- ○
- ○
- ○
- ○
- ○
- ○
- ○

23 THURSDAY
- ○
- ○
- ○
- ○
- ○
- ○
- ○
- ○

24 FRIDAY
- ○
- ○
- ○
- ○
- ○

November
2023

25 SATURDAY
- ○
- ○
- ○
- ○
- ○
- ○
- ○
- ○

26 SUNDAY
- ○
- ○
- ○
- ○
- ○
- ○
- ○
- ○

27 MONDAY
- ○
- ○
- ○
- ○
- ○
- ○
- ○
- ○

28 TUESDAY
- ○
- ○
- ○
- ○
- ○

November
2023

29 WEDNESDAY

○ _____
○ _____
○ _____
○ _____
○ _____
○ _____
○ _____
○ _____

30 THURSDAY

○ _____
○ _____
○ _____
○ _____
○ _____
○ _____
○ _____
○ _____

NOTES

_____
_____
_____
_____
_____
_____
_____
_____
_____
_____
_____

December
2023

01 FRIDAY
○
○
○
○
○
○
○
○

02 SATURDAY
○
○
○
○
○
○
○
○

03 SUNDAY
○
○
○
○
○
○
○
○

04 MONDAY
○
○
○
○
○

December
2023

05 TUESDAY

- ○
- ○
- ○
- ○
- ○
- ○
- ○
- ○

06 WEDNESDAY

- ○
- ○
- ○
- ○
- ○
- ○
- ○
- ○

07 THURSDAY

- ○
- ○
- ○
- ○
- ○
- ○
- ○
- ○

08 FRIDAY

- ○
- ○
- ○
- ○
- ○

December

December
2023

09 SATURDAY

10 SUNDAY

11 MONDAY

12 TUESDAY

13 WEDNESDAY

○
○
○
○
○
○
○
○

14 THURSDAY

○
○
○
○
○
○
○
○

15 FRIDAY

○
○
○
○
○
○
○
○

16 SATURDAY

○
○
○
○
○

December
2023

17 SUNDAY

○
○
○
○
○
○
○
○

18 MONDAY

○
○
○
○
○
○
○
○

19 TUESDAY

○
○
○
○
○
○
○
○

20 WEDNESDAY

○
○
○
○
○

December
2023

21 THURSDAY

○ _____
○ _____
○ _____
○ _____
○ _____
○ _____
○ _____
○ _____

22 FRIDAY

○ _____
○ _____
○ _____
○ _____
○ _____
○ _____
○ _____
○ _____

23 SATURDAY

○ _____
○ _____
○ _____
○ _____
○ _____
○ _____
○ _____
○ _____

24 SUNDAY

○ _____
○ _____
○ _____
○ _____
○ _____

December
2023

25 MONDAY

○
○
○
○
○
○
○
○

26 TUESDAY

○
○
○
○
○
○
○
○

27 WEDNESDAY

○
○
○
○
○
○
○
○

28 THURSDAY

○
○
○
○
○

December
2023

29 FRIDAY

○
○
○
○ .
○
○
○
○

30 SATURDAY

○
○
○
○
○
○
○
○

31 SUNDAY

○
○
○
○
○
○
○
○

NOTES

www.ingramcontent.com/pod-product-compliance
Lightning Source LLC
Chambersburg PA
CBHW052114020426

42335CB00021B/2753